THE
OCEAN
WE SHARE

Written and Illustrated
by Fauziah Rochman

To the future generations,
love our ocean

My father is a fisherman in the South China Sea. He leaves everyday before sunrise for a day of fishing. The ocean provides a living my family depends on.

I am a clownfish. I live in between the corals of the Java Sea. Sea anemones provide shelter for my family. The ocean is our home, where we live safely and happily.

I am a green sea turtle. My siblings and I were just born on a beach in Australia. Today is my first dip into the sea. The ocean is where I will spend most of my life. I know my life will be wonderful.

I am a starfish. I am shy so I hide under sand or rocks. I wait until the moon comes out to enjoy the night sky. It is the loving Indian Ocean that takes care of me.

I am a mother emperor penguin.
My family depends on me for food.
Together with the other mothers, we
hunt fish in the cold Antarctic Ocean.
The ocean provides all the nutrients
we need to grow and stay warm.

I am an African fish eagle. Watching the ocean from above is my favourite thing to do. My wings let me hover in the air and plunge down into the waters. The ocean is my safe haven.

Seagulls like me go wherever there is food. I can be found along coastal areas all around the world. As winter comes, I fly south to places like South America, where it is nice and warm.

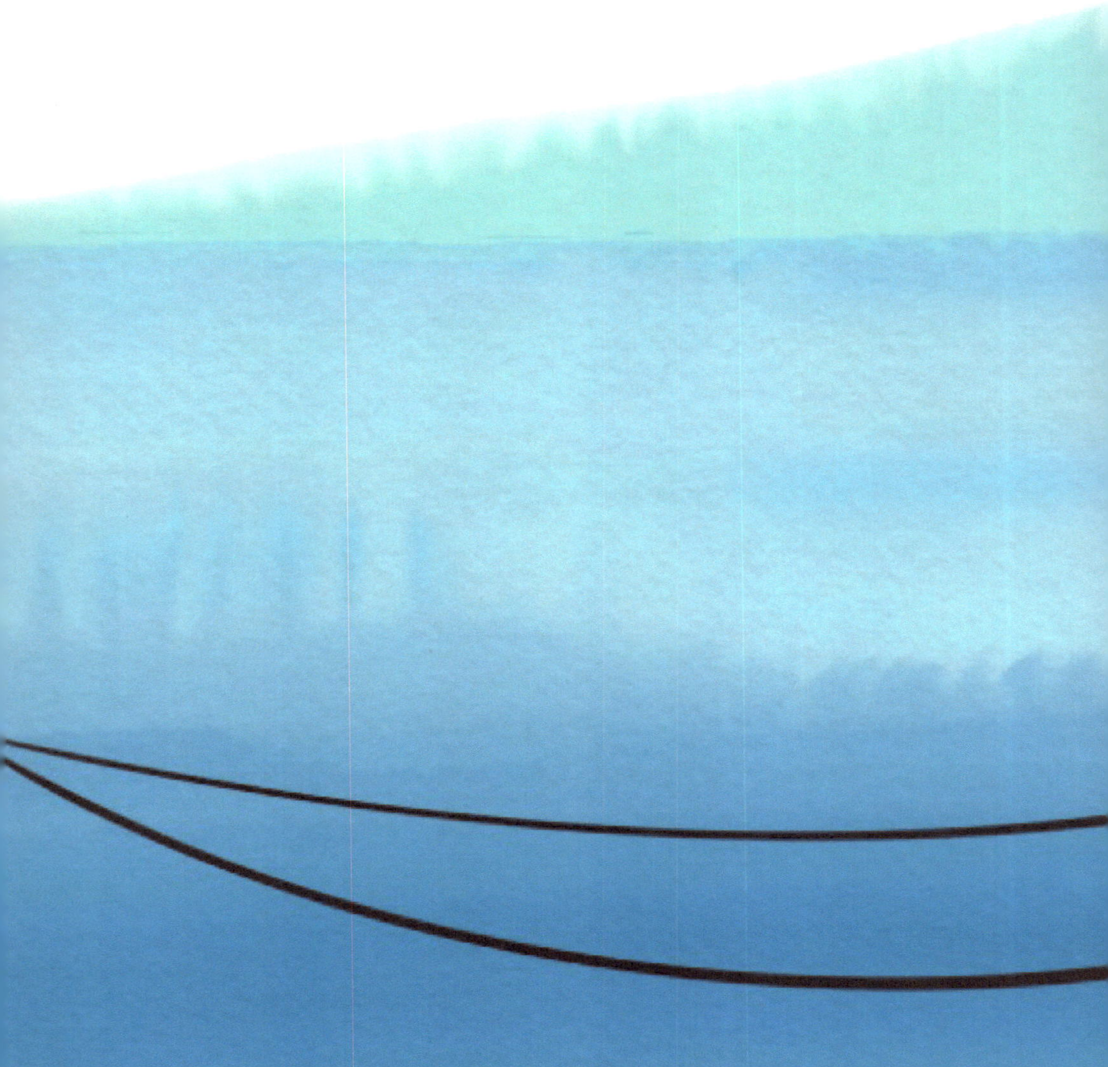

My orca whale family lives in an inseparable pod. We swim freely around the Pacific and Arctic Oceans. The ocean has all we need with its clean water and endless bounty. Nothing can replace our home.

The Pacific Ocean may seem quiet from above. But underneath, jellyfish like us bloom and flourish. As a group, we stay together and protect each other. It is the ocean that harbours us, allowing us to have a beautiful life together.

It is dusk and the breeze blows hard.
I see more and more litter washed up
on my beach. As I patiently wait for my
father to return, I try keeping my beach
clean. It is my promise to take care of
my home.

At night, the busy ocean is now silent.
It rests, and hides its beauty.
The beautiful ocean is ours.
It is home for everyone.

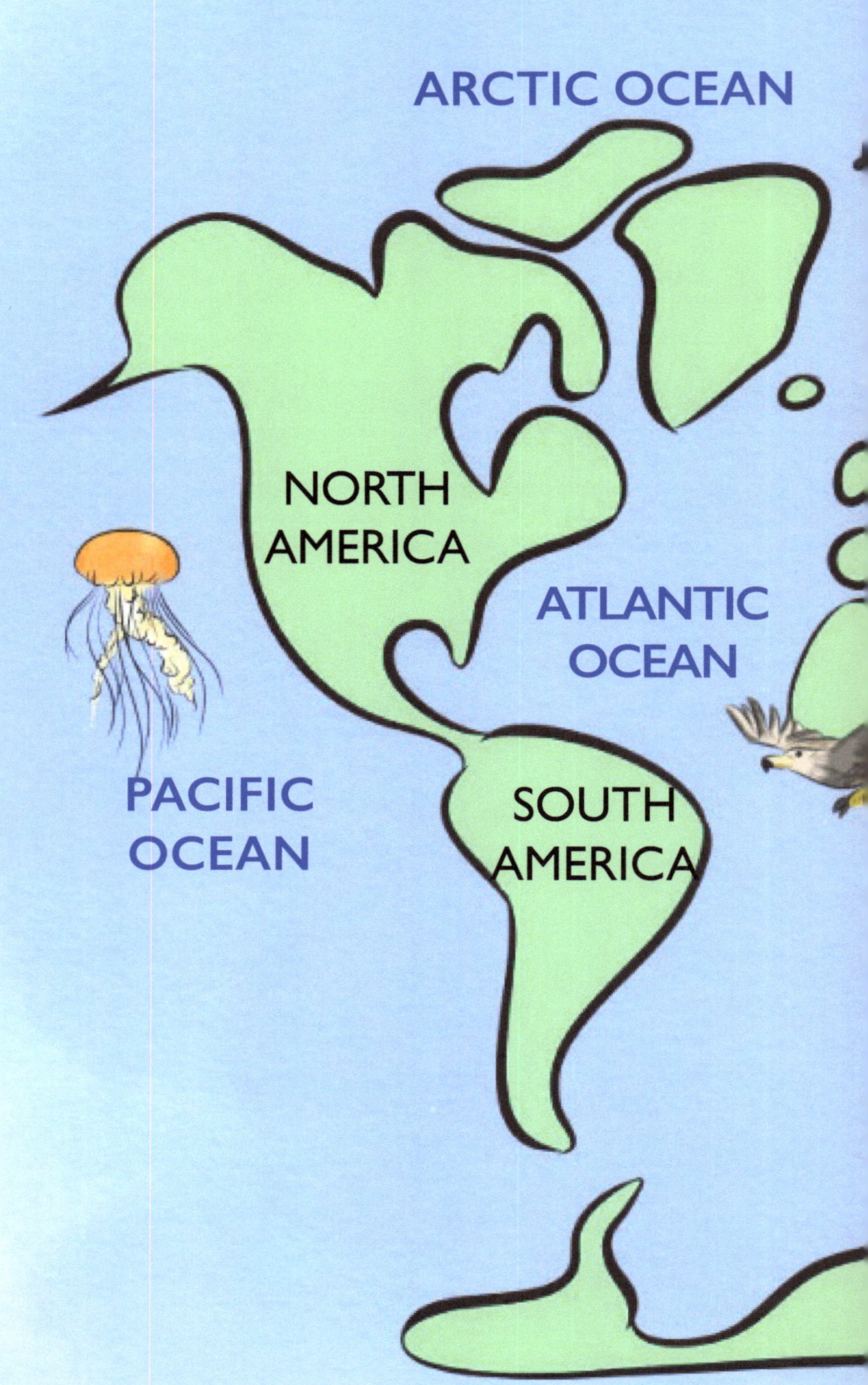

ARCTIC OCEAN
NORTH AMERICA
ATLANTIC OCEAN
PACIFIC OCEAN
SOUTH AMERICA

EUROPE
ASIA
AFRICA
INDIAN
OCEAN
AUSTRALIA
ANTARCTICA

ABOUT THE AUTHOR

Fauziah Rochman is an enthusiastic scientist and environmentalist who is passionate about spreading the joy of science to the public, particularly to children. Coupled with her love for art, she aims to raise environmental awareness in an exciting way. She has graduate degrees from Yale and the University of Calgary in Environmental Sciences. Currently, she lives with her family in Canada. In her free time, she likes to paint and draw. The illustrations in her books are her original work.

OTHER BOOKS BY THE AUTHOR

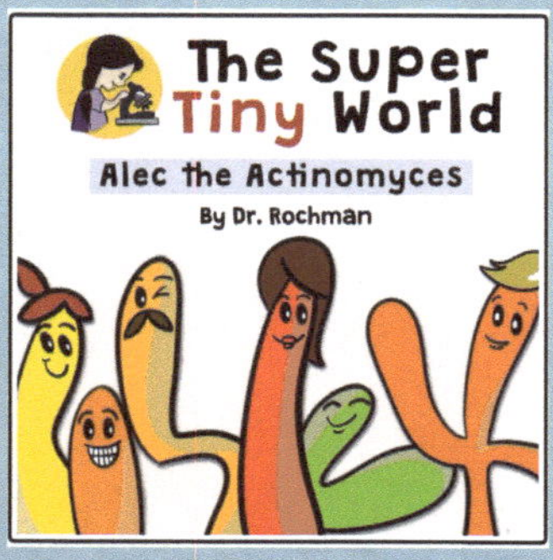